DK Eye Wonder

Invention

LONDON, NEW YORK, MUNICH,
MELBOURNE, and DELHI

Written and edited by Caroline Bingham
Designed by Laura Roberts
Additional design Jane Horne
and Helen Chapman
Editorial assistance Fleur Star

Publishing Manager Susan Leonard
Managing Art Editor Clare Shedden
Jacket design Chris Drew
Picture Researcher Harriet Mills
Production Shivani Pandrey
DTP Designer Almudena Díaz
DTP Assistant Pilar Morales
Consultant Roger Bridgman

First published in Great Britain in 2005 by
Dorling Kindersley Limited
80 Strand, London WC2R 0RL

A Penguin Company

2 4 6 8 10 9 7 5 3 1

Copyright © 2004 Dorling Kindersley Limited, London

A CIP catalogue record for this book
is available from the British Library.

ISBN 1-4053-0599-1

Colour reproduction by Colourscan, Singapore
Printed and bound in Italy by L.E.G.O.

Discover more at
www.dk.com

Contents

4-5
How to be an inventor

6-7
From then to now

8-9
Early inventions

10-11
The Industrial Revolution

12-13
On the water

14-15
Full steam ahead

16-17
On the road

18-19
In the air

20-21
Blast off!

22-23
In the kitchen

24-25
Everyday things

26-27
A new material

28-29
Electricity

30-31
The telephone

32-33
Photography

34-35
A world of sound

36-37
... and vision

38-39
Medicine

40-41
Write it down!

42-43
Computers

44-45
Into the future

46-47
Glossary and Inventors

48
Index

How to be an inventor

Have you ever thought of something that would make your life easier, or more fun? A time machine? A robot? Whatever your invention is, to be successful, lots of other people will have to want it too.

Small beginnings
Some inventions seem accidental. Take the Post-it® note. Art Fry needed something to bookmark his church hymn book. He hit on the idea of using paper notes with a new glue a colleague, Dr Spencer Silver, had developed.

One invention sparks another

Your invention doesn't have to be a new idea. You could improve on something that already exists. James Dyson didn't invent the vacuum cleaner. He invented the bagless vacuum cleaner – one that many people want to buy.

Early vacuum cleaners were huge.

This cleaner had to be pumped by hand – an awkward operation.

The Star was lightweight, but it still needed hand pumping.

The first upright cleaner collected dust in its canvas sack.

The Dyson bagless cleaner was a huge development.

1902   1908   1911   1920   1986

Never give up!
The electric light bulb is an invention that really changed the world. But it didn't come easily. Thomas Edison thought it would take six weeks to develop, but instead it took more than a year. He famously claimed: *"I have not failed... I have just found 10,000 ways that will not work."*

Many people tried to invent the light bulb. Edison and Joseph Swan were the most successful.

4

Protect your invention

Once you have a brilliant invention, you must patent it to show that it was your invention, so no one else can say it was theirs. Patent applications are granted for a certain number of years.

This is a model of the Wright Flyer.

Patent for the Wright Flyer – the first granted for a flying machine.

Another way

Draw a diagram of your invention and write all about it, then post all the information to yourself. The letter will get a date stamped on it in the post, which proves you thought of it before that date. But remember, do not open it!

Remember, keep the envelope sealed and keep it safe!

The bat rests safely on two plastic clips while a hook holds the glove and ball.

Eureka?

● Many patent applications are never developed, like the one for a ladder to help spiders climb out of the bath.

● Other patents include a nappy for a pet bird, and one for an inflatable rug. You can file a patent for all sorts of ideas.

A child inventor

At the age of nine, Austin Meggitt invented a device to hold his baseball equipment on the front of his bike. He filed his invention at the US Patent Office in 1998.

Austin called his invention the "glove and battie caddie".

5

From then to now

Fossils suggest that early humans used tools.

It is fascinating to take a look at the inventions that have changed our lives over the centuries. Just imagine life without wheels, or light bulbs, or any of the other things that make life easier.

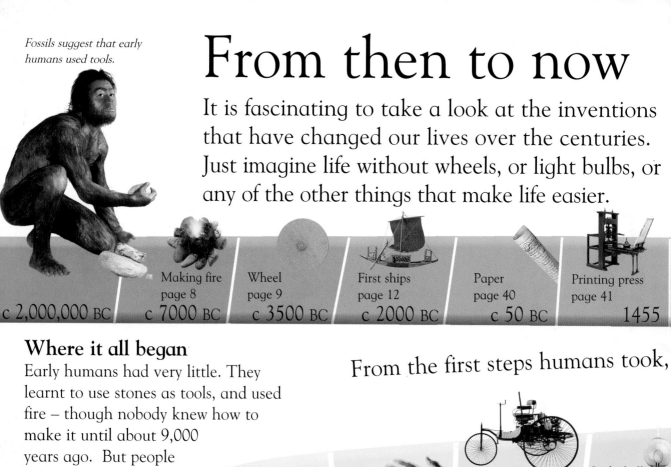

Making fire page 8	Wheel page 9	First ships page 12	Paper page 40	Printing press page 41
c 2,000,000 BC	c 7000 BC	c 3500 BC	c 2000 BC	c 50 BC	1455

Where it all began
Early humans had very little. They learnt to use stones as tools, and used fire – though nobody knew how to make it until about 9,000 years ago. But people are quick learners.

From the first steps humans took,

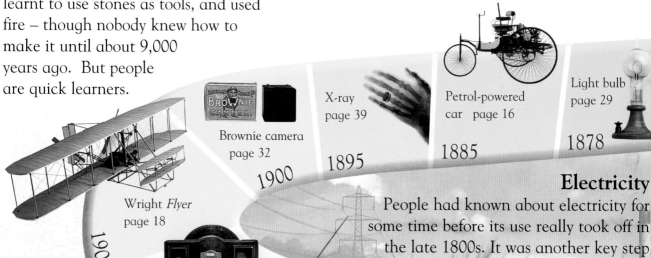

Brownie camera
page 32

X-ray
page 39

Petrol-powered
car   page 16

Light bulb
page 29

1900

1895

1885

1878

Wright *Flyer*
page 18

1903

Electricity
People had known about electricity for some time before its use really took off in the late 1800s. It was another key step to the modern world.

Televisor
page 36

1926

Sputnik 1
page 21

1957

1971
Microprocessor

Personal computer
page 43

1977

The microprocessor
The microprocessor was yet another huge leap for humankind. Without its invention, personal computers would have been an impossible dream.

The Industrial Revolution

The modern world really began with the birth of the factory during the Industrial Revolution. The factory brought together workers and powered machinery, and so speeded up production.

Spinning jenny
page 10
1764

1700s
Industrial
Revolution

Improved steam engine   page 10
1769

Hot-air balloon
page 18
1783

First photographic image   page 32
1826

people have never stopped inventing.

Stephenson's *Rocket* page 14
1829

1800s
Electricity

Phonograph
page 35
1877

Box telephone
page 30
1876

Refrigerator
page 22
1834

What's next?

All sorts of people invent objects that make our lives comfortable, or more fun. Some inventions are simple, others the result of years of research by huge companies. We can only imagine what the future holds.

Mobile phone
page 31
1979

Space shuttle
page 20
1981

Compact disc
page 35
1982

Internet
page 43
1983

At first, fire came from sparks.

Early inventions

Many of the things around us were invented thousands of years ago. These are the things whose invention was essential to life as we know it: the control of fire, farming, clothing, tools, and transport.

From an open fire...

to fire in a box.

Strike a light
Fire has been used for thousands of years, but it was not until the invention of the match in the 1800s that people had a portable, safe, and easy source of fire.

Stone saws didn't work very well.

Changes
The long-handled axe hasn't changed much since its first appearance. The obvious different is that a stone head has been replaced with forged metal.

Serrated edge

It's all in the edge
Like the axe, the main improvement to the saw came with a metal blade. But the basic design, with its serrated, jagged edge, stayed the same.

7000 BC	6000 BC	4000 BC	3500 BC
Making fire Earliest example found in Europe	Axe Earliest example found in Sweden	Plough First used in Sumeria	Wheel Earliest example found in Mesopotamia

8

Ploughs like this were used 4,000 years ago.

The first ploughs were made of wood.

Power brings change

Farmers used ploughs in ancient Egypt to turn the soil ready for planting, but they used wooden ploughs pulled by oxen. Today's tractor has the power of hundreds of oxen.

Today's ploughs are made from metal.

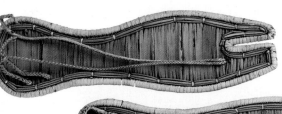

That's more comfortable!

Do you wear trainers? They are probably made from plastics and rubber. Early people used the materials around them to protect their feet – such as the reeds used for these Egyptian sandals.

Solid and small

Some early wheels were made from solid discs of wood. Before that logs had sometimes been used as rollers.

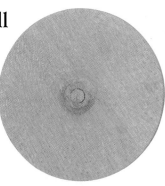

Strong but heavy

Wheels made of three planks held together by struts became more common, and are still used in some areas of the world.

Getting lighter

Spokes first appeared when sections were cut out to lighten the weight. It made lightweight chariots possible.

New materials

The discovery that rubber and metal could be used for wheels brought about a wheel strong enough to carry a car.

2000 BC	2000 BC	1500 BC	1827

Spoked wheel Earliest example found in Mesopotamia	Saw Earliest example found in Egypt	Shoes Earliest example found in Mesopotamia	Matches John Walker England

The Industrial Revolution

The Industrial Revolution began in Britain in the 1700s and gradually spread to Europe, taking new ideas and methods of doing things. It was an important time. One area of huge change was the cloth industry.

Cloth is woven on looms.

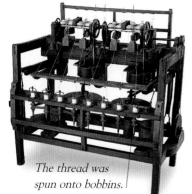
The thread was spun onto bobbins.

We need more thread

The 1700s saw the invention of machines that wove cloth more quickly. The water frame, powered by water, speeded up the making of the thread.

Keep on weaving

Steam-powered looms first appeared in the 1780s. Edmund Cartwright, inventor of the power loom, actually had no experience of weaving. He just saw a way to improve it.

An injection of power

The discovery that steam could be harnessed and used to power machines speeded up industry. The first steam engine sucked floodwater out of mines, allowing more coal to be mined.

The steam turns wheels and cogs.

Steam engines gradually appeared in the cloth industry.

1733	1764	1769	1769 
Flying shuttle John Kay England	Spinning jenny James Hargreaves England	Improved steam engine James Watt Scotland	Water frame Richard Arkwright England

The rise of the factory

As machines were invented that needed power sources, so factories were built to put them in. People had to come to the factory instead of working from home.

Factories created pollution.

SMASH IT UP!

Not everybody welcomed the new machines. In the early 1800s a group of people went around smashing them up. They were known as the Luddites. By 1816 they had given up. The machines were here to stay!

An important metal

Another major invention in the 1700s was the increased production of iron. Iron could now be used in ways never before dreamed of.

This factory is powered by water driving a big waterwheel.

Spinning machines

A changing landscape

The Industrial Revolution also saw huge changes in everyday structures. This iron bridge, the first in the world, is still in use today. The first iron buildings were also put up.

 1770
Factories
Richard Arkwright
England

 1779
Spinning mule
Samuel Crompton
England

 1779
Iron bridge: Abraham Darby (builder) & Thomas Pritchard (designer), England

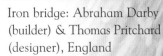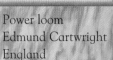 1785
Power loom
Edmund Cartwright
England

11

On the water

Thousands of years ago, someone wove a large basket, covered it with animal hide, and used it as a boat. This was a coracle. That person would be amazed at the variety of boats and ships that sail the seas today.

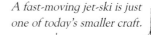
A fast-moving jet-ski is just one of today's smaller craft.

Slow-moving coracles are still in use today.

Reed boat
Some of the earliest boats were made from reeds. People making these boats did so where there was no supply of wood.

Even the sail was made of reeds.

Speed it up
The Phoenicians are believed to have developed the double-decked "bireme", a ship that allowed for twice as many oars as before.

Chinese junks amazed explorers with their single steering oar rudders.

6000 BC		2000 BC		1100 BC		1200	
Reed boat Egypt		First ships Egypt		Oars Phoenicians Eastern Mediterranean		Rudder China	

SS Great Britain

This incredible ship was the first of its kind. It was a triumph for its designer, Brunel. It was the first steamship built of iron, and the first ship built as a luxury liner.

A man of vision

Isambard Kingdom Brunel designed three extraordinary ships in the 1800s, using the latest technology of the time.

The Queen Mary 2 is the largest ship afloat.

Big for its time

If you'd lived in the 1200s, your first sighting of a Chinese junk would have left you speechless. These were the largest ships in the world.

SS Great Britain had a six-blade propeller. Previous ocean-going ships had side paddle wheels.

A modern giant

This gigantic ship can carry 2,620 passengers, with 1,253 crew. It is more than three and a half times the length of the *SS Great Britain*.

1807	1845	1955	1973
The *Clermont* Robert Fulton USA	*SS Great Britain* Isambard Kingdom Brunel England	Hovercraft Christopher Cockerell England	Jet-ski Clayton Jacobsen USA

13

Full steam ahead

Horses had been pulling wagons along tracks since the 1550s. As steam power developed, some forward-thinking inventors began to imagine the benefits of steam locomotives replacing the horses.

George Stephenson

George Stephenson invented a train and railway line that really worked; not bad for a man who had no schooling and couldn't read until he was 19.

The first steam train

History was made as Richard Trevithick's steam locomotive chuffed slowly along a cast-iron track. The train managed 8 kph (5 mph), but it was so heavy it broke the rails.

Chimney

The *Rocket*

George Stephenson and his son Robert built the *Rocket* – the engine that finally proved to people that trains were faster and stronger than horses. It went a record-smashing 48 kph (30 mph), easily beating any other locomotives at the time. The railway age had arrived!

The pistons move up and down as steam is forced in and out.

Steam travels along this pipe to the pistons.

Boiler – water boils and makes steam.

Firebox – fire heats water in the boiler.

The driver stands here and shovels coal into the firebox.

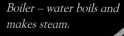

The wheels move round as the pistons pump up and down.

1769	1804	1825	1829
Efficient steam engine James Watt Scotland	The first steam locomotive Richard Trevithick England	First railway – Stockton and Darlington England	The *Rocket* George & Robert Stephenson England

Making tracks

The first railway opened in 1825. It ran for 43 km (27 miles). You can now travel 10,214 km (6,346 miles) from Russia to North Korea without changing trains!

A train wheel's lip, or flange, helps to prevent derailment.

How does it work?

Steam pumps the pistons up and down. The pistons are joined to the front wheels, so this makes them turn.

Water barrel

Coal is stored here.

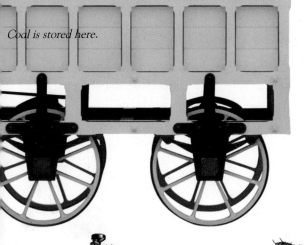

US use wood

Early US steam locomotives burnt wood instead of coal. The frame at the front of this train pushed cattle off the track.

An 1880s woodburning train

It's electric

This electric locomotive is an early version of today's high-speed trains. Overhead cables or a third rail supply the power.

Early electric train

Diesel power

Diesel-electric engines need less servicing than steam trains. They also don't need overhead cables like electric trains do.

The Burlington Zephyr

The future

High-speed electric trains are already used instead of planes for short journeys in Japan, France, and Germany. People tend to prefer them.

The Japanese Bullet train

1832	1879	1897	1964
Woodburning train Baldwin locomotive works USA	Electric locomotive Werner von Siemens Germany	Diesel engine Rudolf Diesel Germany	The *Bullet* train Central and West Japan Railways, Japan

On the road

Before the invention of the car, people used horses to move any great distance – or they walked. Yet today many people could not lead the lives they do without this machine.

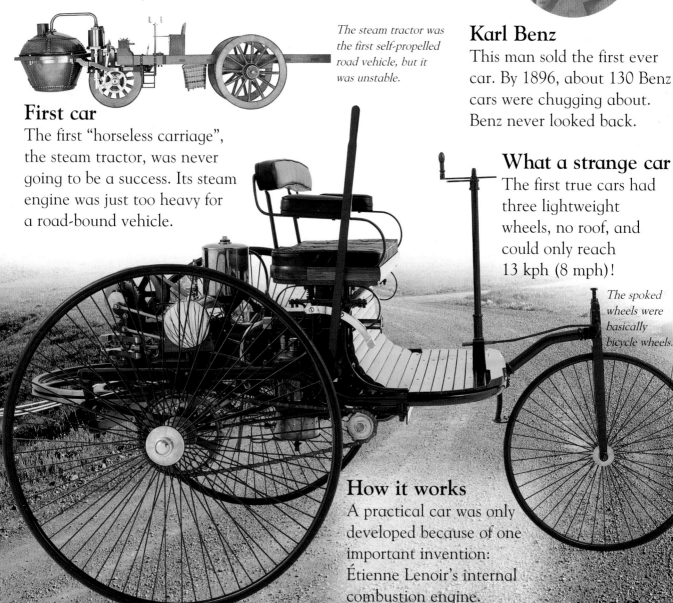

The steam tractor was the first self-propelled road vehicle, but it was unstable.

First car
The first "horseless carriage", the steam tractor, was never going to be a success. Its steam engine was just too heavy for a road-bound vehicle.

Karl Benz
This man sold the first ever car. By 1896, about 130 Benz cars were chugging about. Benz never looked back.

What a strange car
The first true cars had three lightweight wheels, no roof, and could only reach 13 kph (8 mph)!

The spoked wheels were basically bicycle wheels.

How it works
A practical car was only developed because of one important invention: Étienne Lenoir's internal combustion engine.

1769	1859	1885	1891
Steam tractor Nicolas Cugnot France	Internal combustion engine Jean Joseph Étienne Lenoir France	Petrol-powered car Karl Benz Germany	Four-wheel car Émile Levassor France

Internal combustion engine

An internal combustion engine burns fuel inside cylinders after an electrical spark is sent to start the fuel burning. Its invention led to smaller engines.

The four pistons suck in a mixture of fuel and air.

A spark ignites the mixture of fuel and air.

A new craze

The Benz *Velo* was the first car to sell in significant numbers. It looked a little like a horse carriage.

A car for all

Ford introduced the mass production of cars, which made them cheaper. By 1927 more than 15 million *Model T*s had been sold.

On the road now

The cars we use today are powered by petrol, but one day petrol will run out so we need to find an alternative source of power.

A possible alternative

This car has fuel cells that are powered by hydrogen. The owner has to buy tanks of liquid or gaseous hydrogen.

WARNING! CAR COMING!

The Red Flag Act of 1865 said that three people had to be in charge of a "horse-less vehicle" in England: two on board and one in front with a red flag. The vehicle could only travel at 3 kph (2 mph) in towns.

1893	1908	1959	1999
Licence plate France	*Model T* Ford Henry Ford USA	Modern seat belts Nils Bohlin Sweden	Fuel-cell (hydrogen) car Daimler-Chrysler USA

In the air

People dreamed of taking to the skies for hundreds of years, but the first aeroplane did not take off until the 1900s. Imagine how incredible that first flight was for its inventors, the Wrights.

Cluck, quack, baa

The first creatures to fly in a man-made craft were a duck, a cockerel, and a sheep. They were sent up in a hot-air balloon by the French Montgolfier brothers.

An early dream

Wilbur and Orville Wright grew up fascinated by flight. They longed to find a way that they could achieve it.

The long narrow wings had a slight curve.

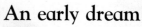

The first flight lasted for 12 seconds. The Flyer rose about 3 m (10 ft).

A movable rudder helped the steering.

The pilot lay on the lower wing.

Let's try again!

This is a replica of the Wright Brothers' *Flyer*, the first aeroplane. The *Flyer* was the result of years of experiments and failures. Yet the Wrights refused to give up.

An elevator moved the nose up or down.

The *Flyer* was made of wood and cloth.

1505	1783	1853	1903
Leonardo da Vinci draws flying machines Italy	Hot-air balloon Montgolfier brothers France	Glider George Cayley England	Wright *Flyer* Orville and Wilbur Wright USA

The first successful single-rotor helicopter flight.

Sikorski R-4
1945

It works on paper...

The first idea for a helicopter was sketched by Leonardo da Vinci 500 years ago, but it took until 1940 to make a successful machine. Today's helicopters can fly at speeds of up to 400 kph (250 mph).

A jet success

This little aircraft was one of the first aeroplanes to be fitted with a jet engine. Jet engines speeded up air travel and paved the way for longer flights.

Gloster E28/39

Concorde

Speed queen

Concorde's appearance in the 1970s was exciting because it was the fastest passenger aeroplane in the world. It has travelled from New York to London in less than three hours.

Boeing 747 (jumbo jet)

Getting bigger

The Superjumbo is far larger than the jumbo jet, currently the world's largest passenger plane. It will seat up to 555 passengers, on two decks running its full length.

A380 (Superjumbo)

1930	1940	1969	2006
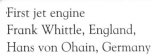		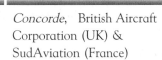	
First jet engine Frank Whittle, England, Hans von Ohain, Germany	Single rotor helicopter Igor Sikorsky Russia/USA	*Concorde*, British Aircraft Corporation (UK) & SudAviation (France)	Superjumbo A380 Airbus consortium Europe

Blast off!

Glance into the night sky and you may be lucky enough to see a satellite as it passes overhead. Yet the discovery that we can blast into space is a recent one.

Rocket facts

- The first living creature in space was a dog called Laika. She was sent up in 1957.
- Many of the inventions around us were developed for use in space. Smoke detectors were first used on *Skylab*!
- *Sputnik 1* was 58 cm (23 in) wide.

Rocket man

Robert Goddard got little praise when his liquid-fuelled rocket shot upwards in 1926, but it was a key moment in the history of space travel.

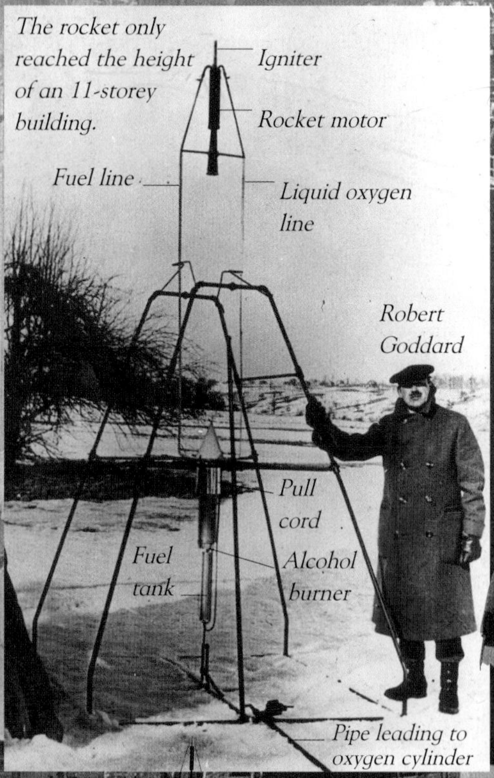

The rocket only reached the height of an 11-storey building.
Igniter
Rocket motor
Fuel line
Liquid oxygen line
Robert Goddard
Pull cord
Fuel tank
Alcohol burner
Pipe leading to oxygen cylinder

USA

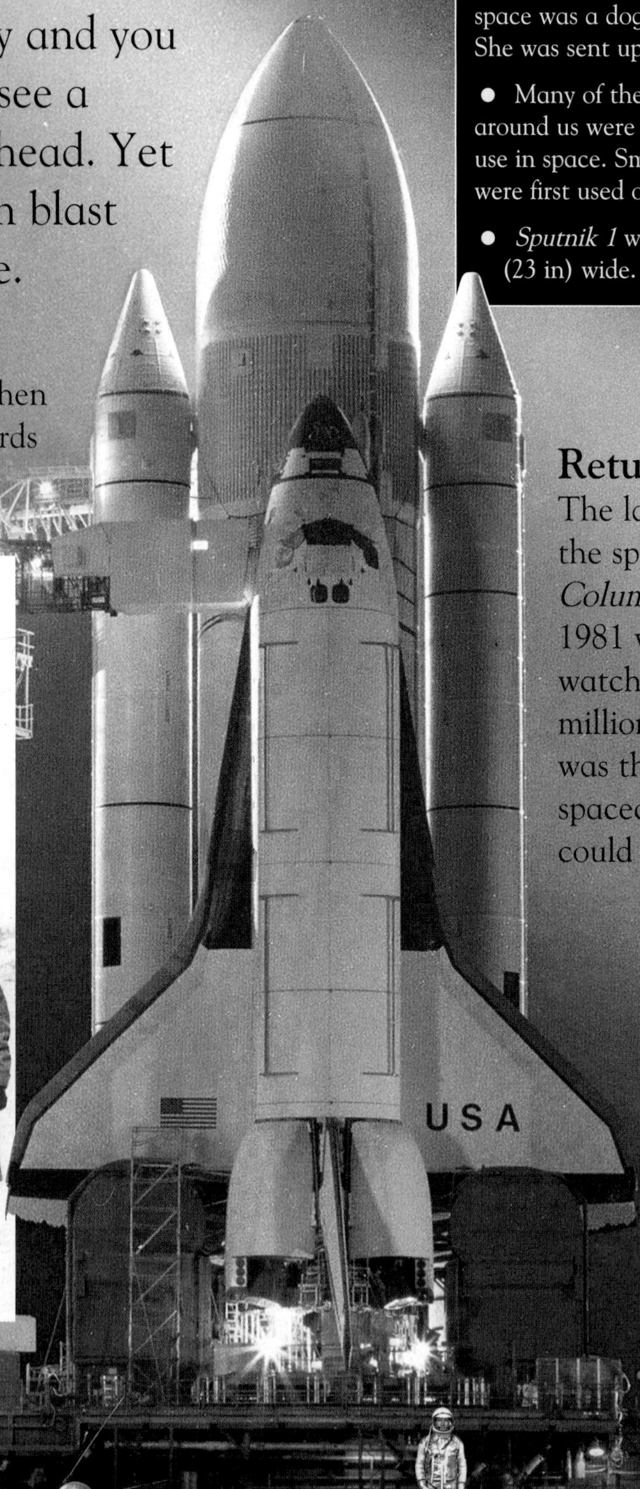

Return trips

The launch of the space shuttle *Columbia* in 1981 was watched by millions. This was the first spacecraft that could be reused.

1926	1957	1959	1973
Liquid-fuelled rocket Robert Goddard USA	*Sputnik 1* Valentin Glushko & Sergey Korolyov, USSR	Space suit B.F. Goodrich Company USA	Space station NASA USA

Sputnik 1

Sputnik 1 was the world's first man-made satellite. At little more than the weight of an adult human, this Russian invention was tiny – yet it took just 98 minutes to orbit the Earth.

Sputnik *sent a continuous "beep, beep" signal back to Earth.*

One of four radio antennae.

Nine astronauts lived on Skylab *before it was abandoned in 1974.*

Getting dressed for space

Before people could travel into space, they needed special clothing. The first space suit was invented in 1959. It was hard and uncomfortably heavy.

A life in space

The first people to live successfully in space were those on board the space station *Skylab. Skylab* was launched in May 1973.

Skylab *collected power from the sun by means of its solar panels.*

The *Hubble* space telescope has more than 400,000 parts.

Let's get closer!

Hubble was designed to send back clearer images of far-off planets and galaxies than could be obtained from Earth. The idea was first suggested in 1946 by Dr Lyman Spitzer.

1981	1984	1990	2004
Space shuttle NASA USA	Manned maneuvering unit (MMU), NASA USA	*Hubble* telescope NASA USA	*Pathfinder* on Mars NASA USA

In the kitchen

Have a good look in your kitchen. When do you think the cooker was invented, and what about the fridge? What about things like tea bags, or margarine? Everything has a history!

You could buy an expensive car for the price of the first microwave.

Gas stove, c 1910

Electric refrigerator, 1934

A slow start

Zachaus Winzler gave dinner parties in Austria in 1802 using a gas cooker, but the idea didn't spread until James Sharp began making cookers in 1826.

A cold start

The first practical refrigerator was built by Jacob Perkins in 1834, but like many inventors, he didn't push his machine, and others developed it.

A happy accident

Percy Spencer was studying radar when he felt a sticky mess in his pocket. The radar microwaves had melted a peanut bar, and he'd found a new way of cooking.

1810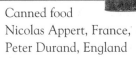
Canned food
Nicolas Appert, France,
Peter Durand, England

1826
Gas stove
James Sharp
England

1834
Refrigerator
Jacob Perkins
USA

1869
Margarine
Hippolyte Mège-Mouriés
France

A shaky start

Fancy eating a mixture of beef fat, cow's udder, milk, and pig's stomach? Well, that's what went into the first margarine. It got a prize for being the first butter substitute!

Fancy a cuppa?

It is believed that tea bags were invented when a tea merchant began sending out tea samples in silk bags. People poured boiling water over the bag... and ordered more.

The first toaster for the home was called the Toastmaster.

"Now! A toaster so simple, even a child can operate it!"

Has it popped yet?

Charles Strite was so fed up of burnt toast that he invented a pop-up toaster in 1919, but the first toasters didn't appear in the home until 1926. People loved them.

At one point, the inventor of sliced bread tried holding the slices together with hat pins!

A long wait

It took 16 years for Otto Rohwedder to produce a sliced bread that didn't go stale. He invented a machine that sliced and wrapped the loaf.

1908	1919	1928	1946
Tea bag Thomas Sullivan USA	Pop-up toaster Charles Strite USA	Sliced bread Otto Rohwedder USA	Microwave oven Percy LeBaron Spencer USA

Soap helps oil and water mix.

Everyday things

Take a look around you. What things do you use every day? We all wash and clean our teeth, and perhaps you have a pair of jeans. Where do you think these things first came from?

Animal bristles

No dirt on me!

Soap was originally made from a boiled mixture of animal fat and wood ashes. It certainly didn't smell very good. Many soaps still contain animal fat, but the ashes have been replaced – and perfume added.

A pig has its uses

Have you ever felt the back of a pig? Pig hair is stiff and scratchy, and before the 1930s it was ideal for making the bristles of a toothbrush. The handle was made from bone.

Bone handle

The name "zip" came from the sound of the zip being opened and closed.

Zip it up!

Whitcomb Judson got so bored of lacing his boots that he invented a boot fastener. This early zip didn't work properly, but Gideon Sundback improved it, and the zip as we know it was born.

c AD 150	c 1280	1767	1873
Soap	Spectacles	Jigsaw	Jeans
Romans	China or Italy	John Spilsbury	Jacob Davis and Levi Strauss
Italy		England	USA

I see more clearly now

Like many things, it's hard to know who invented spectacles, but we do know that they were in use in the 1200s.

Early spectacles had no arms and were hinged.

A pair for life?

Hardwearing and tough, jeans were developed as a result of a rush for gold in the USA in the 1800s. This picture shows one of the first pairs produced.

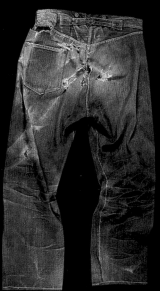

Stripes provided side support to the world's first trainer, launched in 1949.

I didn't know that!

That ridged rubber sole on your trainers began life in 1971 when an American athlete poured molten rubber into a waffle iron. Don't try this at home!

That goes there

The first jigsaw puzzle was made from a handpainted map. It was used to teach children geography.

First teddy

"Teddy's bears" were first sold by a New York shop owner after an American president, Theodore "Teddy" Roosevelt, refused to shoot and kill a bear cub.

What shall we make?

These colourful plastic bricks have only been around for about 50 years. The name LEGO® comes from the Danish words *leg godt*, meaning "play well".

Down... up, down... up

The yo-yo is believed to be the world's second oldest toy after the doll, but it's so old that nobody really knows when it first appeared. Like the doll, it is popular everywhere.

1902	1914	1949	1958
Teddy bear Morris Michtom USA	Zip Gideon Sundback Sweden	Trainers Adolf "Adi" Dassler Germany	LEGO® Godtfred Christiansen Denmark

Celluloid billiard balls tended to explode on impact.

A new material

How many things can you think of that are made of plastic? Did you know that there are many different varieties of man-made, or synthetic, plastics? Their invention changed the world.

It started with a ball...

The discovery of the first usable plastic, celluloid, happened because of the search for a new material to make billiard balls.

The basic ingredients of PVC are...

Oil Salt Water = PVC plastic

Expanded polystyrene keeps heat in, stopping burnt fingers.

These PVC dolls date from the early 1950s.

A slow starter

It took 100 years to find a polystyrene that was stable enough to use. Most people know things made from expanded polystyrene, but did you know that cd cases are polystyrene in its pure form?

Expanded polystyrene is made from foam pellets.

Ready for rain

The material used for your raincoat, PVC, was first created in 1872, but the real leap forward was made by Waldo Semon in the 1920s. He found a way to make it flexible.

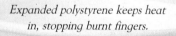

1839	1869	1872	1905
Polystyrene	Celluloid	PVC (polyvinyl chloride)	Bakelite™
Eduard Simon	John Wesley-Hyatt	Eugen Baumann	Leo Baekeland
Germany	USA	Germany	Belgium/USA

A real winner

Most plastics soften with heat, others, like Bakelite™, set rock hard. After its discovery, Bakelite was moulded into all sorts of items, including thermos flasks, clocks, statues, and telephones.

"Dr West's Miracle Toothbrush" was the first with nylon bristles.

Better than pig hair!

Invented by an American chemist called Wallace Carothers, nylon was first used for toothbrush bristles. Nylon has been a hugely successful plastic.

Dr. WEST'S 69¢

Polythene

This was formed in an experiment that went wrong. Its inventors were delighted – here was a new plastic that was a perfect insulator and could be easily moulded. This large balloon is polythene sheet tubing.

Polythene bags don't decompose when thrown away.

Natural gas

Fluoride

Teflon™

The slipperiest, strangest plastic ever?

Plastic facts

• Plastics take different forms. For example, vinyl is used to make hard pipes, but it is also used for plastic wrap.

• Man-made spandex fibres (Lycra™) will stretch to five times their length, then return to their original form.

From saucepans to space

Teflon's heat-resistance and slipperiness makes it ideal for non-stick saucepans. It was also used to coat the Apollo spacesuits. It was discovered by chemist Roy Plunkett when the gas he was testing wouldn't come out of its container. He found it had coated the inside.

1933	1934	1938	1959
Polyethylene (polythene) Eric Fawcett & Reginald Gibson, ICI, England	Nylon Wallace Carothers USA	Teflon™ Roy Plunkett USA	Spandex fibre (Lycra™) Joseph C Shivers USA

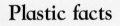

Electricity

The inventions surrounding the discovery of electricity have changed our world. In some areas of the world it is hard to imagine life without electric lighting, or without the power for telephones, televisions, and computers.

The metal Eiffel Tower *in France is a magnet for lightning strikes.*

Don't try this!
In 1752, Benjamin Franklin flew a kite during a thunderstorm, having tied a key to the kite string, to test his idea that lightning was electricity. Luckily he survived!

A safe route
Franklin's experiment led to his invention of the lightning conductor. This is basically a metal rod placed at the top of buildings to attract lightning and divert it to the ground.

Volta's invention was known as the Voltaic pile.

Discs of wet paper were sandwiched between two different metals.

A pile of energy
Once scientists learned more about electricity, they tried to make it themselves. Alessandro Volta managed to invent a means of producing and storing electricity. It was the first battery.

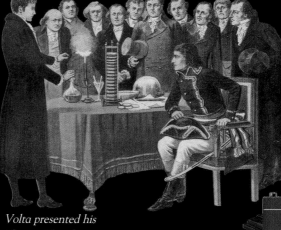

Volta presented his ideas to Napoleon.

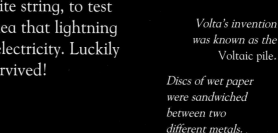

Modern battery

1752
Lightning conductor
Benjamin Franklin
USA

1800
Voltaic pile (the first battery)
Alessandro Volta
Italy

1821
Electric motor
Michael Faraday
England

1831
Generator and transformer
Michael Faraday
England

Calico

Iron

_Coils of
copper wire_

_Swan invented the
glass bulb. Edison
found a filament
that would last
for a long time._

_Thomas
Edison_

Edison's light came with a
warning: "Do not attempt
to light with a match"!

Getting safer

Michael Faraday invented
the transformer. This
important piece of equipment
converts high voltage
electricity to low voltage,
making it safer to use.

Whose bulb?

Light bulbs were invented
at about the same time in
two different countries, by
Thomas Edison in America
and Joseph Swan in England.
It was a long process.

Light facts

● When electricity passes
through a conductor, the
conductor can glow. In a bulb,
this is called a filament.

● Edison tried and rejected
many materials for his
filament, including wood, cork,
grass, rubber, and human hair.

Power for all

Power stations make
enormous quantities of
electricity to run all the
things we need electricity for.

1878	1881	1882	1888
Light bulb Joseph Swan, England, Thomas Edison, USA	Hydroelectric power England	Commercial power station, and electricity meter Thomas Edison, USA	Wind turbine Charles Brush USA

29

The telephone

Before the invention of the telephone, people got in touch by letters that were carried by horses. With the telephone, people were able to talk instantly for the first time. But it didn't happen overnight.

Who invented it?

Alexander Graham Bell has always been credited with the invention of the telephone, but there is a lot of evidence that an Italian-American, Antonio Meucci, got there first.

Telegraph poles connected cities.

The first telephone

Early telephones used a combined mouthpiece and earpiece. Someone spoke into the horn and their voice was changed into electrical signals. Bell's first words were to his assistant, Mr Watson.

"Mr Watson"

The back was originally hidden in a box.

Horn-shaped mouthpiece and earpiece.

Where did the voice go?

The messages were carried along a network of wires, at first held away from the ground by telegraph poles. Some were later routed underground. Before this, telegraph poles had been used to transmit tapped messages.

Bell got people interested in his box telephone by giving many talks and demonstrations.

1876	1879	1889	1900

Box telephone Alexander Graham Bell Scotland	Wall-mounted phone Thomas Edison USA	Automatic telephone exchange Almon B Strower, USA	Candlestick phones Europe/USA

Is that the operator?

In the 1880s, anybody making a telephone call had to go through an operator at a telephone exchange. This made private calls impossible because the operator could listen in. The first automatic telephone exchange appeared in 1891.

Wall-mounted telephone

By 1879, Thomas Edison had perfected a telephone that had a separate mouthpiece and earpiece. The user turned a handle to ring the operator and make it work.

Candlestick telephone

Many telephones of the early 1900s still had no dial: the connection was made via a telephone exchange. The user lifted the receiver to call the operator.

come here, I want you."

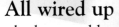

A single fibre can carry thousands of telephone circuits.

Cradle telephone

Telephones like this became popular in the 1930s. Many phones were made of wood or metal, but plastic was appearing.

All wired up

Early telephone cables contained lots of paper-insulated wires contained in a metal casing. Many telephone circuits are now connected by fibre-optic cables.

Mobile telephone

Recognize this? The first mobile phones were so large and heavy that they were called "car phones". They certainly weren't pocket-sized!

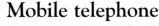

1925	1979	2001	2002
Cradle phones (bakelite) Europe/USA	Mobile phone Bell Telephone Laboratories, USA	US Congress Statute declares Antonio Meucci's part in telephone invention	Camera phones Finland

Photography

In 1826 Joseph Niépce took the world's first photograph. The problem was that he had to leave the camera still for eight hours. Nonetheless, photography had been invented!

The first photograph shows a view of roofs and chimneys.

A plate was put into the back of the camera.

Daguerre's camera

Niépce's colleague, Louis Daguerre, developed his invention and produced an image that did not fade. He called his photographs Daguerreotypes. One problem was that you could only make one copy of the picture.

A new way

At the same time an Englishman, William Fox Talbot discovered a means of taking negatives. These could then be used to make unlimited copies of photographs.

Early Daguerreotypes needed a 3–15-minute exposure time. That's a long time to sit still!

William Fox Talbot

Talbot only looked into photography because he was frustrated by his poor artwork. His discovery was the path to the future of photography.

The camera had to rest on a tripod to keep it steady.

The Daguerreotype was used for a good 20 years before being abandoned.

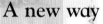

1826	1839	1889	1900
First photographic image	Daguerreotype	Roll film	The Brownie
Joseph Niépce	Louis Daguerre	George Eastman	George Eastman
France	France	USA	USA

Speed it up a little!

Photography still took time and could be uncomfortable to sit for, but in 1851 Frederick Scott Archer introduced the wet-plate process. It made photography far faster. Photographs could be taken in just 30 seconds in bright light.

One rather large problem

In 1900, enlargements could not be made. If you wanted a big picture, the camera had to be big! In 1900, George Lawrence built a mega-sized camera to take shots of a train.

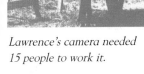

Lawrence's camera needed 15 people to work it.

Photography for all

In 1888 George Eastman invented film that could be rolled and placed inside a simple camera. He called it the Kodak (a word he made up).

The first Kodak camera weighed just over 1 kg (2 lbs).

Just point and snap.

No need for film

Digital cameras work in the same way as television cameras; they don't use film, but make electronic pictures. These pictures are loaded onto a computer, where they can be altered and printed out.

Digital cameras do not use film.

 1931
Electronic flash
Harold Edgerton
USA

 1935
Colour film
Kodak
USA

 1948
Polaroid camera
Edwin Land
USA

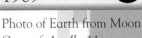 1969
Photo of Earth from Moon
Crew of *Apollo 11*
USA

A world of sound

Today's portable radios show how bulky early radios were.

What is a radio? It brings us music, news, and comedy, and all with the flick of a switch. It is an incredible invention because it keeps everybody in touch with what is happening in the world.

Let's go "wire-less"
The key moment for the invention of radio was the discovery that messages could be sent without the need for wires running from the transmitter to the receiver.

Tall wooden towers held up the wires that sent and received the messages.

Who's he?
Guglielmo Marconi sent the world's first radio messages when he was just 20 years old. He has long been seen as the inventor of radio.

Radio waves were sent from these wires.

The wire-less station
One of Marconi's earliest radio stations, at Wellfleet, Massachusetts, shows how high the masts had to be to send and receive the signals.

Marconi's radio station was pulled down many years ago.

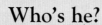

1877	1887	1901	1924
Phonograph Thomas Edison USA	Gramophone Emile Berliner USA	First radio transmission across the Atlantic Ocean Guglielmo Marconi	First message sent from England to Australia Guglielmo Marconi

Sound was recorded on the cylinder.

Edison turned the handle to work the phonograph.

A record player has a needle on the end of an arm.

Say that again, please

Progress with recorded sound came a little earlier than that with radio. The first recorded words, "Mary had a little lamb", were made by Thomas Edison on his phonograph.

From records...

A vinyl record stores sound in grooves. The record can be played using a needle, which vibrates between the walls of the groove.

Recorded music came out of the gramophone's horn.

to tapes...

A cassette tape stores sound in magnetic patterns. A tape recorder reads these.

Audio cassette tape

Play that again

The gramophone was invented by German engineer Emile Berliner. Music could be recorded onto flat discs and played back, again and again.

Compact disc

to cds...

A compact disc, a cd, stores sound in tiny pits on its surface. It is read by a laser.

The user had to turn a handle.

MP3 player

to MP3

MP3 allows music to be copied from the Internet, organised, and stored in a computer's memory.

Early discs were made of shellac, a gummy substance that oozes from some insects.

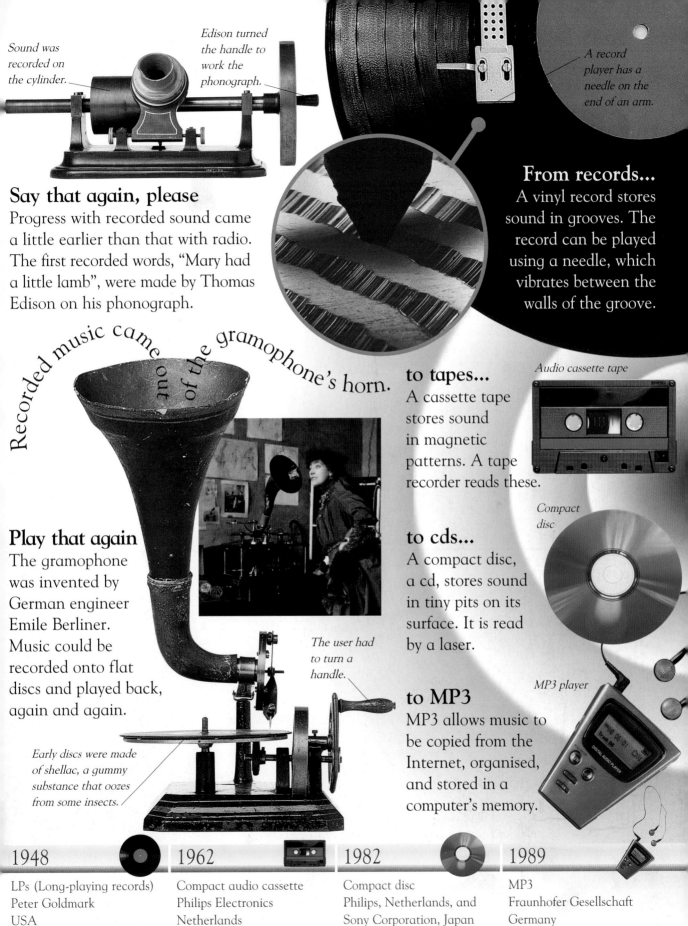

1948	1962	1982	1989
LPs (Long-playing records) Peter Goldmark USA	Compact audio cassette Philips Electronics Netherlands	Compact disc Philips, Netherlands, and Sony Corporation, Japan	MP3 Fraunhofer Gesellschaft Germany

... and vision

Imagine that you have never seen television. One day, in a large shop, you see a "televisor". On its tiny screen is a flickering image of a face. This is what greeted amazed shoppers in a famous shop in London, England, in 1926.

Baird-vision

Scotsman John Logie Baird televised the first moving image with his televisor. Although this machine was not used for long, Baird's public demonstrations fired people's enthusiasm for television.

Inside the televisor's wooden casing was a large spinning disc.

Let's buy a televisor!

About 1,000 televisors were made between 1926 and 1934. However, one of its problems was that the picture and the sound could not be seen and heard together. Many people thought television had no future.

Baird used a spinning Nipkow disc in his televisor.

Stooky Bill

Stooky Bill

The first image that John Logie Baird transmitted was that of a dummy's head that he called Stooky Bill. His first machine was made from a hatbox, torch batteries, bits of old wood, and knitting needles.

1884	1897	1926	1953
Nipkow disc	Cathode ray tube	Televisor	First colour TV broadcast
Paul Nipkow	Ferdinand Braun	John Logie Baird	USA
Germany	Germany	Scotland	

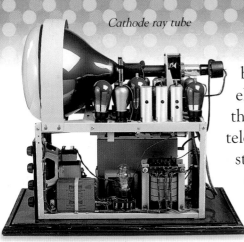

Cathode ray tube

Inside a television

The cathode ray tube has been at the heart of electronic televisions since they began to replace televisors in 1936. This strange-looking object changes electricity into the pictures that we see on the screen.

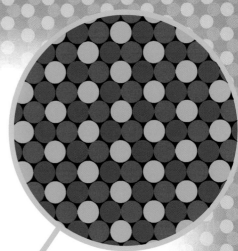

Coloured dots

The picture you see on your television screen is made up of 625 lines. The colour comes from thousands of tiny red, green, and blue dots. The light from these blends together to form all the colours you see on the screen.

"The biggest time-waster of all time."

With just 30 scan lines, the televisor produced a weak image.

This is a television from the 1950s, when colour televisions were beginning to appear.

New developments

Today's flat-screen televisions don't used cathode ray tubes. Instead, liquid crystals display the picture on the screen.

1955	1956	1977	1988
First portable TV	Remote control	Pocket TV	LCD television
Ekco	Robert Adler	Clive Sinclair	Sharp
England	USA	England	Japan

Medicine

People have always practised medicine. Early people used herbs, and the ancient Chinese invented acupuncture. But many of the medical instruments we use were not invented until surprisingly recently.

Get the point

Vaccines are medicines that stop people from catching diseases. Today we inject vaccines, but when first discovered they were simply wiped onto a cut because syringes had not been invented.

This 19th-century inhaler was used to send patients to sleep before surgery.

Ether-soaked sponges.

Numb that pain

Before the discovery of anaesthetic to knock somebody out, many patients having surgery had to be tied or held down. The first anaesthetic was a liquid called ether.

The surgeon sees inside the patient and controls the robotic arms from this workstation.

Lister's use of antiseptic spray helped to keep operating theatres germ-free.

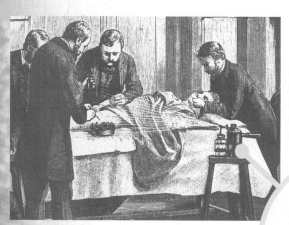

Preventing infection

Doctors in the mid-1800s did not know that germs on dirty clothes, hands, and equipment caused disease. Fortunately, along came Joseph Lister with his antiseptic spray, which killed germs.

1798	1819	1846	1866
Vaccine	Stethoscope	Anaesthetic	Clinical thermometer
Edward Jenner	René Laënnec	William Morton	Thomas Allbutt
England	France	USA	England

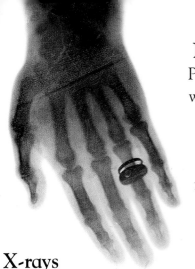

It began with a mould

Penicillin, the first antibiotic, was discovered by Alexander Fleming. He was growing bacteria when he noticed some had been killed by a mould. He used the mould to make penicillin. It was later developed by Ernst Chain and Howard Florey.

X-rays

The German physicist who produced the x-ray image above of his wife's hand was staggered by his accidental invention. Here was a way of seeing through skin.

Dead bacteria surround the penicillium.

Penicillium mould

The robotic arms are operated by remote control.

A particular penicillium mould is used to make the penicillin antibiotic.

Robotic help

Some surgeons today use robots to perform operations. The surgeon then has three, steady robot hands to use, which can work through smaller cuts in the patient. This means that there is less pain for the patient, and it takes less time to heal.

This is a magnified picture of the penicillium mould.

1867	1895	1921	1999
Antiseptic Joseph Lister Scotland	X-rays Wilhelm Röntgen Germany	Band aids Earle Dickson USA	Robotic surgical system Intuitive Surgical, Inc. USA

Write it down!

Do you keep a diary? You certainly write notes at school. Keeping records in this way is something that would be impossible without the invention of something to write on – paper – and something to write with – pencils and pens.

Bushy top

Green outer rind

The inner fibres are used to make papyrus sheets.

Strip by strip

About 5,000 years ago the ancient Egyptians discovered how to use papyrus, a waterside reed, to make parchment. Strips of the inner fibres were laid down, then a second layer was pressed on top. The result was dried in the sun.

Reed pens were dipped in an ink made of soot and glue.

It flies across the page!

Believe it or not, some early pens were made from goose feathers and called quills. The tip was sharpened to a point, and the quill pen dipped in ink. Quill scribes produced beautiful writing.

The tip was sharpened and slit.

The hollow feather only held a small amount of ink.

We have paper

Paper was invented in China some 2,000 years ago, but its invention was actually kept a secret for 700 years. Paper can be made from the fibres of certain plants, and from cotton or linen rags.

c 3100 BC	c 3000 BC	c 220 BC	c 50 BC
First writing Sumeria	Papyrus Egypt	Standardised Chinese writing China	Paper China

Pencil
The "lead" inside a pencil is actually made of graphite (a form of carbon), combined with clay.

Ballpoint pen
The tiny ball inside a ballpoint pen's nib rolls as you write, taking ink from the pen onto the page.

Felt-tip pen
The nib of a felt-tip pen is made of nylon fibres, which soak up ink from the pen's body.

Printing then
Hand lettering was slow. Things speeded up with the invention of the printing press. Whole pages of a book could now be set up and inked from movable type.

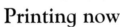

Movable type is reversed. It prints the right way around.

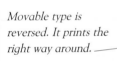

Setting type   *Printing press*

Printing now
Most books and newspapers today are printed on massive machines called web presses. A book is designed on a computer, and then printed on a large sheet of paper, which is later cut up into pages. It is much faster than hand lettering or using movable type!

c AD 500	1455	1565	1938
Quill pen Europe	Letterpress printing Johann Gutenberg Germany	Pencil Conrad Gesner Germany	Ballpoint pen Ladislao and Georg Biró Hungary

41

Computers

Computers are special machines and their invention has changed our world. They are used for numerous tasks, from booking holidays and designing books to guiding aeroplanes.

Charles Babbage

Babbage is sometimes called the "father of computing". His plans for calculating machines were very advanced, but they were never fully built because he ran out of money.

Moving on

The Difference Engine would have had an estimated 25,000 parts. Babbage went on to invent a machine that did have many characteristics of a modern computer.

A part of Babbage's Difference Engine No. 2 was built in 1991. It worked perfectly.

Was this the first computer?

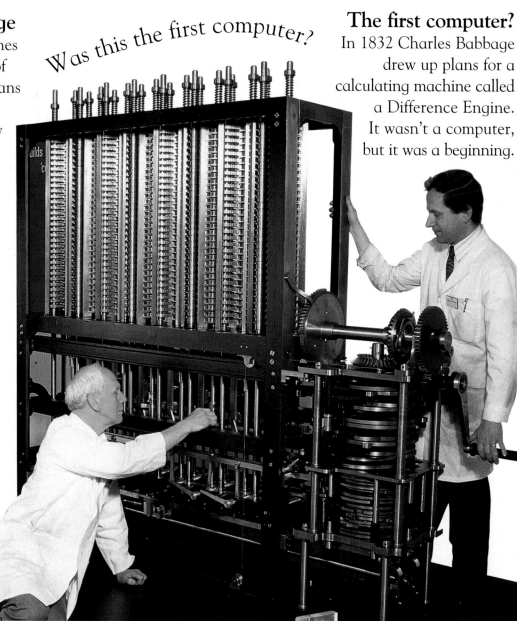

The first computer?

In 1832 Charles Babbage drew up plans for a calculating machine called a Difference Engine. It wasn't a computer, but it was a beginning.

1832	1945	1947	1958
Difference Engine Charles Babbage England	*ENIAC* United States Army USA	Transistor J. Bardeen, W. Brattain, and W. Shockley, USA	Integrated circuit Jack Kilbey, USA

The birth of *Eniac*

The first all-purpose electronic computer, *Eniac*, filled a large room. It depended on 18,000 glass tubes called valves, which led to overheating problems.

The Internet began as a means of linking military computers.

The Internet now links millions of computers.

A new solution

The invention of the transistor got around the problem of valves. It is basically an electronic on-off switch, and it led the way to making things smaller, and cheaper.

First transistor

Silicon chip

Today's computers contain millions of transistors placed on tiny slices of silicon. With the invention of the silicon chip, or integrated circuit, computers got even smaller.

Some silicon chips are so tiny that an ant can pick them up.

The Internet

The Internet allows computers all around the world to link up to each other. It provides an easy, quick, and cheap method of communication.

This will sell it!

It's an interesting fact that the first computer game, *Space War*, was invented to help sell a computer. The computer had a circular screen.

1965	1971	1977	1983
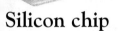 Computer mouse Doug Engelbart USA	Microprocessor Ted Hoff USA	Personal computer Stephen Wozniak and Steve Jobs, USA	Internet J. C .R. Licklider, Larry Roberts, USA

Into the future

What inventions will appear in the next hundred years? What would you like to see? The inventions of the future are ready and waiting for somebody to come along and unlock their secrets.

It looks so real!
Scientists are working on a TV image that can be watched in 3D. You'd be able to walk around the image and see it from different angles.

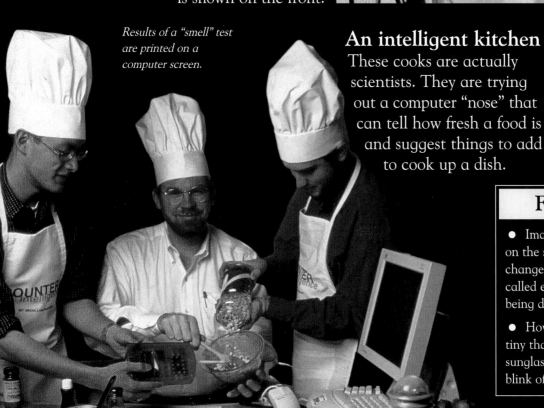

Make me invisible
This clever invention makes it appear as if its wearer is see-through. A tiny camera films what is going on behind the wearer's back, and this is shown on the front.

Results of a "smell" test are printed on a computer screen.

An intelligent kitchen
These cooks are actually scientists. They are trying out a computer "nose" that can tell how fresh a food is and suggest things to add to cook up a dish.

Future facts

● Imagine pressing a button on the spine of a book to change the text inside. It's called electronic text, and it's being developed right now.

● How about a computer so tiny that it's built into a pair of sunglasses. Be online in the blink of an eye!

The future of transport?

One hundred years ago, the first aeroplane had just taken to the skies. Who knows what the future of transport will be – perhaps we will have traffic jams in the sky!

Teeny tiny robots

Nanorobots may be one of the major inventions to come in medicine. These will be so tiny that they can attack infections from inside the body.

Diseased human cell

Nanorobot

In the future we could be driving flying cars!

Help at any cost?

One day, robot companions may be a part of every home... but not yet. This little helper may be able to walk and sing and kick a ball, but it would cost as much as a luxury car.

Glossary

Here are the meanings of some words it is useful to know when learning about inventions.

Antibiotics medicines that work by killing bacteria.

Battery a container that uses chemicals to store electricity.

Electricity a form of energy that is used to provide heat and light, and to power all sorts of machines.

Fuel something that can be burned to give heat, such as petrol for a car engine.

Industrial Revolution a period of rapid change, which began in the 1760s and saw the birth of factories, powered machinery, and an increasing use of iron.

Internal combustion engine a machine inside which fuel burns to create power.

Jet engine an engine that takes in air from outside, heats it up, and pumps it out again to push itself forwards.

kph this stands for "kilometres per hour", a measurement of an object's speed.

Orbit the path an object takes as it circles a larger body. Man-made satellites orbit Earth.

Paddlewheel huge wheels with paddles that were used to move boats and ships before the invention of the propeller.

Patent a document granted by a country's government stating that a person is the first to invent something. It protects their rights to that invention.

Propeller a shaft fitted with blades that spins to move a ship or propeller plane.

Radar a way of using radio to detect objects that are not in sight.

Receiver the part of a machine that collects sound or signals.

Rocket a machine that carries its own fuel and oxygen so that it can propel itself through space.

Silicon a dark grey, hard substance that looks rather like metal but is not a metal. It is used to make silicon chips.

Steam-powered a machine that works because of the power of steam, produced when water boils.

Technology the methods used to make objects and machines.

Transmitter the part of a machine that sends sound or signals.

Inventors

Most of the inventors found in this book are listed here, along with the page number on which they can be found, the dates of their birth and death, and their invention.

Archer, Frederick Scott 33
1813-1857   Wet-plate photography

Babbage, Charles 42
1791-1871   Calculating machines

Baird, John Logie 36
1888-1946   Televisor

Bell, Alexander Graham 30
1847-1922   Telephone

Berliner, Emile 35
1851-1929   Gramophone

Brunel, Isambard Kingdom 13
1806-1859   New uses of iron, including ships and bridges

Carothers, Wallace 27
1896-1937   Nylon

Cartwright, Edmund 10
1743-1823   Steam-powered loom

da Vinci, Leonardo 19
1452-1519   Artist, inventor, and scientist

Daguerre, Louis 32
1787-1851   Daguerreotype

Dyson, James 4
1947-   Bagless vacuum cleaner

Eastman, George 33
1854-1932   Roll film

Edison, Thomas 4, 29, 31, 35
1847-1931   Edison patented more than 1200 inventions, including the electric light bulb and the phonograph

Faraday, Michael 29
1791-1867   Transformer

Fleming, Alexander 39
1881-1955   Penicillin

Franklin, Benjamin 28
1706-1790   Lightning conductor

Goddard, Robert H 20
1882-1945   Liquid-fuelled rocket

Lenoir, Étienne 16
1822-1900   Internal combustion engine

Lister, Joseph 38
1827-1912   Antiseptic

Marconi, Guglielmo 34
1874-1937   Radio transmissions

Meggitt, Austin 5
1988-   Glove & battie caddie

Meucci, Antonio, 30
1808-1896   Telephone

Montgolfier, Joseph and Etienne 18
1740-1810 (Joseph); 1745-1799 (Etienne)   Hot-air balloon

Niépce, Joseph Nicéphore 32
1765-1833   First photographic image

Perkins, Jacob 22
1766-1849   Refrigerator

Röntgen, Wilhelm 39
1845-1923   X-rays

Spencer, Percy 22
1894-1970   Microwave oven

Stephenson, George 14
1781-1848   The Rocket

Swan, Joseph 4, 29
1828-1914   Electric light bulb

Talbot, William Fox 32
1800-1877   Negative photographic images

Trevithick, Richard 14
1771-1833   Steam locomotive

Volta, Alessandro 28
1745-1827   Voltaic pile (the first battery)

Walker, John 9
1781-1859   Matches

Watt, James 10
1736-1819   Improved steam engine

Wright, Wilbur and Orville 18
1867-1912 (Wilbur); 1871-1948 (Orville)   First aeroplane

Index

aeroplanes 18-19
anaesthetic 38
antiseptic 38
audio cassette 35

battery 28
boats 12-13

camera 6, 32-33
canned food 22
car 6, 16-17, 44-45
compact disc 7, 35

Difference Engine 42

electricity 7, 28-29

factory 10-11
fire 6, 8

gas stove 22
Gramophone 34, 35

helicopter 19
hot-air balloon 7, 18
hovercraft 13
Hubble 21

Industrial Revolution 7, 10-11

internal combustion engine 16, 17
Internet 7, 43
iron 11

jeans 24, 25
jet-ski 12, 13
jigsaw puzzle 24, 25

LEGO™ 25
light bulb 4, 6, 29
LPs 35

margarine 22, 23
matches 8, 9
microprocessor 6, 43
mobile phone 7, 31

paper 6, 40
patent 5
pen 41

pencil 41
penicillin 39
personal computer 6, 43
phonograph 7, 34, 35
photograph 7, 32
plastic 26-27
plough 8, 9
printing press 6, 41

radio 34
refrigerator 7, 22
robots 39, 45

ships 6, 13
shoes 9

space shuttle 7, 20, 21
space suit 20, 21
spectacles 24, 25
spinning jenny 7, 10
Sputnik 1 6, 21
steam engine 7, 10, 14
Stephenson's *Rocket* 7, 14

telephone 7, 30-31
television 36-37
televisor 6, 36
toaster 23
tools 8
toothbrush 24, 27
trainers 25
trains 14-15

vaccine 38
vacuum cleaner 4

wheel 6, 8, 9
Wright *Flyer* 5, 18-19

x-ray 6, 39

zip 24, 25

Aibo, a robot dog invented by Sony, Japan

Acknowledgements

Dorling Kindersley would like to thank:
Louise Halsey for original artwork, Pilar Morales for digital artworks, Penny Arlon and Elinor Greenwood for editorial assistance, and Sarah Mills, Karl Stange, and Hayley Smith for picture library assistance.